Nature's Children

WILD DOGS

Tom Jackson

GROLIER
EDUCATIONAL

FACTS IN BRIEF

Classification of Wild Dogs

Class:	*Mammalia* (mammals)
Order:	*Carnivora* (meat-eaters with specialized teeth)
Family:	*Canidae* (dog family)
Genus:	*Lycaon*
Species:	*Lycaon pictus* (African wild dog)

World distribution. Main populations in Namibia, Botswana, South Africa, Tanzania, Zambia, Kenya, and Ethiopia.

Habitat. Grassland and scrubland—from semidesert to alpine. Preference for wooded savanna.

Distinctive physical characteristics. Long, wiry body. Brown fur with white and yellow blotches. White tip to the tail.

Habits. Hunt in packs at dawn and dusk. Roam through large territories and only settle down to breed.

Diet. Small antelopes, impalas, young wildebeests, and zebras.

© 2001 Brown Partworks Limited
Printed and bound in U.S.A.
Edited by Jens Thomas

Published by:

GROLIER
EDUCATIONAL

Sherman Turnpike, Danbury, Connecticut 06816

Library of Congress Cataloging-in-Publication Data

Wild Dogs.
    p. cm. -- (Nature's children. Set 7)
  ISBN 0-7172-5551-4 (alk. paper) -- ISBN 0-7172-5531-X (set)
  1. Wild Dogs--Juvenile literature. [1. Wild Dogs.] I. Grolier Educational (Firm) II. Series.

QL737.C22 W542 2001
599.77'2--dc21

00-067243

Contents

Next time you are out walking and see a dog, stop and look at it for a moment. The dogs that you see in your neighborhood are probably quiet and tame, walking along on the end of a leash. Travel to Africa, though, and you will see an animal that may look like some of the dogs you know, but behaves very differently. It is the African wild dog—a close relation of the domestic pooch, but one that lives as free as the wind and is a skilled and deadly hunter.

There are many different types of wild dog, but African wild dogs have a special place among them. Like lions and other African hunters, African wild dogs hunt the big animals—antelopes, zebras, and wildebeests—that live in the huge, open grasslands of Africa. Hunting is a family business for these dogs. And together, a family of African wild dogs is more daring and more cunning than any other hunters in the world. Keep on reading this book to find out all about these magnificent animals.

Opposite page: *This pack of African wild dogs is hunting on open grassland.*

Relatives

Opposite page:
A coyote from Montana. Coyotes often hunt alone, but they can also hunt in packs just like the African wild dog.

Many thousands of years ago the ancestors of the pet dogs from your neighborhood may have lived very like an African wild dog. All dogs belong to the family of animals called the *canidae*. It is quite a big group of animals, though, and includes dogs that are very different from each other. To keep things simple, scientists put some of the dogs into smaller groups if they are quite similar to each other. The *canis* group of dogs includes the wolves, jackals, coyotes, dingoes, and our own pet dogs. Wild canis dogs are large animals that live in packs (groups) and hunt animals larger than themselves. The two other big groups of dogs are the *vulpes* and *dusicyon*, which are all types of fox.

African wild dogs are different enough from the other types of dog that they are put in their own special group. However, just like the canis dogs, African wild dogs live and hunt together in packs.

Where in the World?

Pet dogs are often called "man's best friend" and can be found most of the places where people live. African wild dogs are only found in a few places. Only a few years ago these animals lived all over Africa south of the mighty Sahara Desert. Now they are mainly found in the huge grasslands of southern and eastern Africa, especially in Namibia, Tanzania, Botswana, and South Africa.

Not only are wild dogs found in fewer places, they are also found in smaller numbers than before. That is because people have chased them off their land and made it hard for the dogs to survive.

Opposite page:
If you want to see an African wild dog in the wild today, the best place to look is southern Africa. There are more dog packs there than in any other part of Africa.

Happy Families

African wild dogs live in friendly family groups called packs. About a hundred years ago the first European explorers in Africa said they saw packs of more than 100 dogs. Today, a pack of 20 animals is thought to be very big.

If you have brothers or sisters that you get along with, you might like the lifestyle of the African wild dog. The packs they live in are made up almost completely of brothers and sisters—usually all the males are brothers, and all the females are sisters. The males and females are never related to each other and always come from different families.

The pack is led by a pair of dogs. They are called the alpha male and the alpha female. These animals often lead the pack when they are out hunting or if they get into a fight with other dogs.

Home on the Range

Have you ever taken a dog for a walk to the park? Dogs like to run around, don't they? Imagine if a dog lived in an enormous park, thousands, maybe millions of times bigger than your local park. Well that is where most wild dogs live—in the rolling grasslands of the Serengeti in Tanzania and Kenya. Wild dogs also live in drier scrubland of southern Africa and the wooded hills of Ethiopia.

A pack of dogs spends most of its time on the move and has no particular home for most of the year. Instead, each pack spends nine months of the year patrolling its range. That is the area where the pack lives and hunts. It can be as big as 580 square miles (1,500 square kilometers). The dogs sleep out in the open during this time, often in very cold, exposed places. The only time they settle down is when it is time for them to breed.

Opposite page: *These African wild dogs live on the wide, open grasslands of the Masai Mara national park in Kenya, East Africa.*

Good Breeding

Pet dogs come in all shapes and sizes. That is because people breed them for particular reasons. Some are bred to be tiny, cuddly lap dogs, others to be big, fierce guard dogs. Wild dogs have not been bred by people. Their body is built in such a way as to make them very good hunters. They are quite tall compared to most other dogs, but wild dogs are not very heavy. That is because they have very wiry bodies with long, slim legs. That makes them fast and efficient runners.

Unlike their close cousin the wolf, wild dogs do not have long noses. Instead, they have blunt snouts that allow them to have a very strong bite. Like other meat-eating animals, wild dogs have many sharp teeth inside their mouth. Some teeth are pointed for ripping meat; others are slicers for chopping up mouthfuls of flesh. Some even act like nutcrackers and are used for cracking bones!

You Can See Me

Wild dogs do not use their sense of smell in the same way that other dogs do. You may have seen pet dogs sniff each other in the street. It is their way of saying "hello." Even though wild dogs have a very good sense of smell, they do not use it to communicate in this way. Instead, they use their other senses of sight, hearing, and touch. When they are hunting, though, sight is their most important sense.

Wild dogs have mainly dark brown or black coats with yellow or white blotches. The blotches make the dogs look like they have been splashed with paint. Each dog has his or her own special pattern so that other dogs can recognize them. Even when the dogs are very far apart, they all know who is who. The white tips on their tails make them particularly easy to see. The dogs use their tails to give each other signals.

Hot Dogs

Wild dogs sometimes get very hot. That is because they live in places where there is no shade. To help them stay cool, they have very large ears. They use them in the same way that an elephant uses its ears to keep it from getting too hot. Hot blood is pumped into the big ears, where it is cooled by the wind. That keeps the rest of the dog's body from getting too hot.

Dogs do not sweat like you or I do when we get too hot. Instead, they pant, blowing out hot breath to cool themselves down. However, this way of keeping cool uses up a lot of water. That can be a problem because for most of the year wild dogs do not have any water to drink. Instead, they get the liquid they need from the food they eat. To save water, wild dogs don't pant until they are very hot indeed—much hotter than other types of dog.

Fast Food

Packs of wild dogs tend to hunt small antelopes, such as impalas, Thomson's gazelles, lechwes, and reedbucks. However, the packs take young, old, or injured wildebeests and sometimes even zebras. These large and fast animals are very dangerous to hunt, and most wild dogs will only do so if there is no easier meat around.

Areas of tropical grassland in Africa often have periods called droughts, when it does not rain. Herds (groups) of antelopes, zebras, and wildebeests get the water they need to live from pools called water holes. During a drought, however, many of the water holes dry out, so the animals spend much of the time moving from one water hole to the next. They often travel many thousands of miles. The wild dogs do not follow the herds when they move, but stay inside their range. Droughts are difficult for the packs since there are not many animals around for them to eat.

Hunting

If they were left on their own, most wild dogs would die. The dogs must live in packs so that they can hunt. Wild dogs hunt in packs of at least six or seven, often more. Their prey (animals they like to eat) live in large herds. The pack usually hunts in the cool of dawn and dusk. The low light at these times makes it hard for the prey to see the dogs coming. When a pack of dogs is out hunting and sees a herd of impalas (their favourite food), it will charge toward them and start the chase.

Wild dogs can run at about 37 miles per hour (60 kilometers per hour) for over 3 miles (5 kilometers). That's usually a lot farther than their prey can run. The pack just follows the weakest prey animal until it is in striking distance. First, a dog runs past the prey and forces it to change direction. Then, a large male bites one of the prey's back legs or its tail, while another leaps up to the prey's face and bites its top lip. This bite usually brings the animal down. The dogs have won.

Opposite page:
These African wild dogs have chased this red lechwe antelope into the water to catch it.

Feeding

Opposite page:
This black-faced impala is "pronking." You can see how it pulls its back legs up and toward its body to keep any hunters from getting hold of them.

The prey animals do not make it easy for the dogs. If a dog misses the prey when it tries to bite it, the dog could easily end up being killed by a kick. Antelopes also "pronk"—leap into the air as they run—in order to make it harder for the dogs to grab their back legs.

When they have caught their prey, wild dogs often begin eating the animal while it is still alive. That is because they are not strong enough to kill their prey outright like a lion would. Instead, the dogs rip open their prey's stomach and start eating while the animal lies dying. This may sound gruesome, but the animal usually dies of shock within seconds. That is less time than it takes a big hunter such as a lion to suffocate its prey.

Robbed!

Packs of wild dog may be good at catching their food, but they are not very good at keeping hold of it. As soon as they have made a kill, big birds called vultures start to circle in the skies above. They are waiting for the dogs to finish eating before grabbing the leftovers. However, the vultures may attract a pride of lions or a clan of hyenas, which will then bully the dogs into giving up their meal. When this happens, the thieves often fight over the meat left by the dogs. There is not always much food left, though. That is because unlike other hunters, wild dogs never fight with each other over their food. They just eat as quickly as possible. That is because they know a lazy lion or some other scavenger (animals that eat food that other animals have caught) may happen along and steal the rest of their meal!

Opposite page:
If they are lucky and no other animal steals their catch, African wild dogs may store some of their food to eat later.

Big Prey, Small Prey

Opposite page: *These wild dogs are about to catch a wildebeest. When they first approach a herd, wild dogs keep their heads down so as not to scare the animals.*

Even though they are quite big compared to most dogs, African wild dogs are still much smaller than the animals they hunt for food. The horns of a wildebeest or a kick from a threatened zebra will often kill a wild dog. Their cousins and neighbors the jackals hunt for much safer small prey such as hares or very young gazelles. So why do wild dogs risk their lives hunting big animals?

A hare weighs about 10 pounds (4.5 kilograms), a wild dog weighs about 55 pounds (25 kilograms), and an adult wildebeest weighs 330 pounds (150 kilograms). That means a pack of six dogs can catch their own weight in food when they catch just one wildebeest. They would need to catch at least five hares each to equal this amount of food if they hunted alone—and that's five times as much work. Hunting large animals in packs can be dangerous, but it saves the dogs time and energy.

Setting Up Home

When it is time to breed, the pack decides to settle down in one place for a while. The breeding season depends on where the pack lives, but it is usually the time of year when there is a lot of food available. The pack takes over a den that has been dug by another animal, such as an aardvark (a type of ant-eater) or a hyena. Anywhere that is deep enough to keep the pups (young wild dogs) warm during the first few weeks of life will do. To make sure that the den is extra snug and warm, the mother dog will line the inside with soft grasses. Sometimes the den may become full of fleas, ticks, and other pests. In this case the pack will have to search out a new den for the mother and her young.

Opposite page: This African wild dog mother has found a sandy den for her young.

Blind and Helpless

A female wild dog is pregnant for about 70 to 73 days. That is a long time for an animal of her size. For the first 50 days the pups do not grow very much inside the mother. That allows her to keep active and help the pack find food. In the last days of the pregnancy, however, the pups will grow very quickly.

Wild dogs produce litters (a group of pups that are born together) of about 10 to 16 pups—that is enough pups for a new pack every year! The pups are born underground and stay there for about a month before coming out into the open for the first time. They are blind for the first three weeks and rely on milk from their mother for all this time.

Growing Up

After the young have been born, the whole pack helps raise them. They are all family after all, so it is just like you helping your mom out if you have a much younger brother or sister. The mother does not go far from her pups for the first month of their lives. The rest of the pack go hunting as usual but bring food for her when they get back. Because they cannot bring back food in their paws, the dogs will cough up some of the food that they have eaten for the mother. The coughing up is called regurgitation. It is important that the mother eats, since otherwise she would not have the energy to feed her pups.

When the pups are old enough to come outside and no longer need their mother's milk, they too eat regurgitated food. They ask an adult to feed them by licking the adult on its lips. After about seven weeks the pups' mother goes back to hunting, and another adult is left to look after them.

Opposite page:
This African wild dog is regurgitating some food for these hungry pups.

On the Move Again

Opposite page: *African wild dog pups may begin to eat meat when they are only five weeks old.*

When the pups are about two months old, they take on the long, wiry body shape of the adults. They also get the same blotchy coloration on their fur. The pups become much more active and begin to join in with the everyday activities of the pack. Pretty soon they try to follow the rest of the pack when it sets out to hunt. At first the pups are led back to the den by an adult, but after a few weeks they are allowed to follow and eat with the adults. Of course, it takes a while for the little pups to catch up with the adults and arrive at the scene of the kill. The adult dogs have been eating since the prey went down; but when the pups arrive, the adults always stand aside and let them eat.

About 10 weeks into the pups' life the pack leaves the den and sets off wandering again. The pups learn hunting skills as they get older, but do not join the hunt until they are about a year old.

Leaving Home

Wild dogs are usually happy living together; but when the pack gets too big, the young dogs start to get in trouble with the alpha male and female. Eventually, they have a huge fight, and a group of either brothers or sisters will leave the pack forever. The dogs that leave will join a group of other wandering brothers or sisters and will start a new pack. In this way the dogs can always make sure that none of the males and females in the pack are related to each other.

It is very dangerous for a dog to be alone and away from the pack. They could die from hunger or be killed by hyenas and lions.

Opposite page:
As long as they stay together with their brothers or sisters, these pups should be safe from enemies.

Hunting School

Opposite page:
If it stays with the pack and learns how to hunt well, this pup may live to be more than 10 years old.

Catching an antelope running at 30 miles per hour (48 kilometers per hour) is not easy. A pack of wild dogs can do it twice a day, day in day out, and still rarely miss a kill. When the pups are young, they spend many months watching the pack hunt to learn what they must do. A pup may catch a hare or rodent when it is growing up; but when it becomes an adult, it must hunt as part of a team.

Some packs are better than others at catching certain types of animals. Most wild dogs only eat impalas and other small antelopes. A few packs have learned how to bring down bigger, more dangerous animals such as zebras. The skills they need to do this, and the knowledge of where to find water and shelter, are taught to the youngsters by the older members of the pack.

Making Friends

Have you ever behaved like a baby to get what you want? Well, sometimes wild dogs do the same. Pups lick the lips of adults if they want some food. When an adult dog wants to be nice to one of the leaders of the pack, it does the same. Scientists think that this babyish behavior makes the pack leaders treat the other members better.

Wild dogs hunt at dawn and dusk, and spend the day resting. At several times during the day the pack members greet each other. It involves them running around excitedly, making squeaking noises, and rubbing their cheeks together. At other times male members and pups enjoy play-fighting.

Opposite page: *Although most play between the dogs is friendly, it is sometimes used to show who is the boss.*

In Danger

Opposite page:
Some people hope that African wild dogs that have been bred in zoos could be released into the wild to create new packs.

The numbers of African wild dogs have been going down fast for a long time. Scientists think there are only 3,000 to 5,000 wild dogs left in the world. That is because most of the places where the wild dogs live have been turned into farms in the last 100 years. Only the national parks are left for the packs to roam and hunt. Unfortunately, the dogs do not know where the park ends and farmland starts. All too often they wander into farmland and attack cattle. Then a farmer may shoot them. One South African farmer shot a pack of 20 dogs that had gotten onto his land. In just a few minutes he had killed 10 percent of that area's wild dogs.

Packs often have to work very hard to survive. Because they cannot live in as many places as before, and there is not as much food around, the packs have had to become smaller and smaller. That makes them more likely to be wiped out by diseases carried by pet dogs, such as rabies or distemper.

Satellite Tracking

Scientists have put African wild dogs on the list of endangered animals. That means the dogs may die out in only a few years if nothing is done. However, all is not lost for these wonderful animals. Conservationists (scientists who try to save endangered animals) have been working to help the dogs for several years. One problem is that the dogs are hard to find because they wander over such a large area. To help them keep track of the dogs, scientists have been using satellites to follow their movements. Scientists are also trying to help keep pet dogs from getting sick, so they can't give their diseases to the wild dogs.

Wild dogs have always been at great risk from animals such as hyenas and lions. But the greatest danger of all to the dogs survival now comes from humans.

Words to Know

Breed To produce young.

Canidae The name of the animal group that all dogs belong to.

Conservationist A scientist who tries to help animals that are in danger of dying out.

Drought A time when it does not rain, and the land dries out.

Herd The name given to a group of large animals such as cows, antelopes, or zebras.

Litter Young animals born together.

Pack A group of wild dogs.

Prey An animal that another animal hunts for food.

Pronk The big "springing" jumps that antelopes make to keep hunters from catching them.

Pup A young wild dog.

Range The big area of land where wild dogs live and hunt.

Regurgitate To cough up food that has already been eaten.

Scavenger An animal that eats the leftovers from another animal's meal.

Scrubland A wide, open dry area of land where only a few scattered grasses and trees can grow.

Snout The nose and jaws of a dog.

Water hole A pool of water where animals gather to drink.

INDEX

Cover Photo: Martin Harvey / NHPA
Photo Credits: John Shaw / NHPA, page 4; David Middleton / NHPA, page 7; H. P. H.
Photography / Bruce Coleman, pages 8, 41; Chris Caldicott / Still Pictures, page 11; Stephen
Krasemann / NHPA, page 12; Martin Harvey / NHPA, pages 15, 37, 45; A. Warburton & S.
Toon / NHPA, page 18; Daryl Balfour / NHPA, page 21; Peter Pickford / NHPA, pages 22, 34;
Dr. Hermann Brehm / Bruce Coleman, page 25; M. & C. Denis-Huot / Still Pictures, pages
26, 29; Nigel J. Dennis / NHPA, pages 30, 33, 38, 42.